Le Tour

a century of the Tour de France

Jeremy Whittle

Foreword by Greg LeMond

First published in 2003 by
Collins, an imprint of
HarperCollins*Publishers*
77–85 Fulham Palace Road
Hammersmith
London, W6 8JB

The Collins website address is www.collins.co.uk

Collins is a registered trademark of HarperCollins*Publishers* Ltd.

09	08	07	06	05	04	03
7	6	5	4	3	2	

Copyright © Essential Works Ltd., 2003

Produced by Essential Works
168a Camden Street, London, NW1 9PT

A catalogue record for this book is available from the British Library.

ISBN 0 00 716594 3

Front jacket: The Tour de France in the Pyrénées, 1938 (Getty Images).
Back Jacket: Greg LeMond, the first American rider to win the Tour de
France (Eamonn McCabe/The Observer/Getty Images).

Printed and bound by Butler and Tanner

Contents

Below: Greg LeMond at the 1986 Tour, on his way to becoming the first American to win the race.

Foreword

Until I was 16 years old I had no idea what the Tour de France was. Back then, an American riding in the Tour – let alone winning it – was about as likely as a Frenchman playing in the World Series. But by the late 1970s I had made it my goal to win the Tour de France before I was 25, something that ultimately I achieved.

I had so much passion for the Tour that I lived for the race – and it was photographs that had fired my enthusiasm, when I was growing up in Reno, Nevada. Cycling came naturally to me, but I still didn't know much about the sport itself; I owe that knowledge to Roland Della Santa, who used to build my bikes and had a big archive of European cycling magazines, such as *Miroir du Cyclisme*. Even though at the time I didn't speak French, I learned about the Tour through them; their photography was very dramatic and through those pictures I started to understand and appreciate the race. Even though everybody told me that I was crazy and that it couldn't be done, winning the Tour became my dream. Although reality can sometimes disappoint your dreams, that wasn't true in this case. The Tour was far greater and far grander than my dreams and never more so than when I experienced it on my first trip to Europe in the summer of 1978. I realized then that even the greatest photography struggles to capture the full scale of the Tour de France.

As a kid, I had got into cycling by a fluke. I was crazy about downhill skiing and when I went to a ski camp in British Columbia they got me riding a bike to lose weight, saying it was the perfect complement to ski training. I loved the speed and adventure of the descents, the time spent exploring the countryside and the equipment, too. I'd never thought about racing, but when I was 14 I rode my first race, in Nevada, in tennis shoes, shorts and a T-shirt – and got second place. The next race I rode, I won. By 1976 I had my beautiful yellow Cinelli bike and a yellow jersey to go with it, without realizing the significance of the colours. Everybody was laughing at me – they all thought that I reckoned I was the Tour de France champion, but, back then, I still didn't know what they were talking about.

Looking back, I can say that my experience of the Tour de France changed my life, because it enriched and shaped it. Winning the Tour – and particularly winning it twice after my hunting accident – made me who I am and helped me understand myself that much better. Last autumn I joined all the surviving Tour champions on a stage in Paris, at the presentation of the 2003 Tour de France route and stood alongside Eddy Merckx and Bernard Thévenet, Charly Gaul and Ferdi Kubler. You will find captured here moments from the races we rode, as we fulfilled our boyhood dreams in our moments of athletic grace.

Of course, every generation of cyclists thinks that it's better than the last, but I realize now that it's the Tour itself that makes champions, and not the reverse. It's the collective heroics of the past one hundred years that have built the legend and fired dreams, the same dreams I had when growing up in Nevada.

Greg LeMond,
Montana, March 2003

Introduction

In the Tour de France you often hear crashes before you see them. Sometimes it's the high squeal of tyres on overheated racing rims, or the cries of alarm from the riders, carrying on the warm summer air. On other occasions, it's the crack of shattered bike frames, or the snap of crumpling wheels.

Oddly, after a while, perhaps as in any other battle zone, you become immune to the suffering. After all, pain and the ability to cope with it is the Tour's *raison d'être*. The riders seem to develop a thicker skin, too, as they crash to the tarmac, howling momentarily with pain, but then, seconds later, they remount their bikes and chase after the big group of riders known as the peloton. They will continue day after day, through the oppressive heat of the Midi or the thin air of the Alps and Pyrénées, glassy-eyed with exhaustion, bloodied from constant falls, skin burned to mahogany, sometimes close to tears. Even in the modern Tour – the televised, commercialized, sometimes ethically compromised Tour – the shame of quitting forces riders to go far beyond normal human limits. So they carry on, strapped, bandaged, patched up and sometimes numbed by dope, in part to keep their sponsors happy, but also because of the huge weight of the sacrifice and suffering that have gone before. Sacrifice, so former Tour director Jacques Goddet once said, is responsible for the Tour's popularity. 'Sacrifice,' asserted Goddet, 'is part of the Tour's legend.'

And so the modern Tour has become a journey to the sacrificial altars that created the myth, a pilgrimage to the remote mountain roads made famous by the sufferance of the past. The Tour's most feared mountain peaks – Galibier, Ventoux, Alpe d'Huez, Tourmalet – are linked together in a century-old chain of pain.

The 2003 Tour celebrates one hundred years of epic endurance and human drama that has characterized the old race since it was first conceived, over a long lunch in a Parisian brasserie, by Henri Desgrange, a French newspaperman and former racing cyclist. Fighting a bitter circulation war in the New Year of 1903, Desgrange, editor of *L'Auto*, was intrigued by the suggestion from his chief cycling reporter, Géo Lefèvre, that the paper should sponsor a bicycle race around France. A cycling Tour de France, mused Desgrange, after a few glasses of wine, as fascinated as he was appalled by Lefèvre's idea. 'Bad roads, thousands of miles of cycling, no matter what the weather…?' he said to Lefèvre. 'They'll all be killed and even the best will take a beating … and have you thought about the costs?'

Yet on January 19, 1903 *L'Auto* announced 'the greatest cycling trial in the entire world', and revealed the inaugural route of mammoth 18-hour stages, some to be ridden in darkness, others in the heat of the day. It was a brilliant, crazed idea: a bike race through the wildest parts of France, on unmade dirt roads, that was sure to attract mavericks, vagabonds and adventurers. The prize money on offer saw to that. The riders would race through the night, their progress checked by spot controls. To heighten the drama, the stages would be absurdly long – from Paris to Lyon, for example, a mere 467 kilometres, or Marseilles to Toulouse, a short jaunt of 423 kilometres.

The first Tour de France, won by Maurice Garin, immediately caught the public's imagination and quickly became a favourite topic of barroom debate. So heated were these debates that brawls soon became commonplace. In 1904 the race became overtaken by controversy as rivalry between betting cartels led to fighting in the streets. At St-Etienne fans and riders started a mass brawl, breaking apart only when a horrified Géo Lefèvre arrived in his car and fired his pistol. As they rode through the dark, some riders were attacked in the hills, pulled off their bikes, beaten and left groaning on the verge, while their rivals sped ahead, towed by a supporter's car. Others found chopped trees blocking their path, or nails strewn across the road. Some even decided that they'd had enough of sitting on their bikes and decided to catch the train.

Much to Desgrange's horror, there was enough skullduggery and deception – cheating, by any other name – in 1904 to fill two filing cabinets in the race organizer's office with complaints. Garin, who was the winner for the second year running, was later disqualified and banned from racing for two years, while the organizers warned that any future trickery would be dealt with severely. Despite being appalled by the levels of chicanery reported to him and declaring the idea of the Tour 'finished', Desgrange opted to continue to stage the race. Late in 1904 he announced, a little pompously, that the Tour would be staged once more as 'a moral crusade for the sport of cycling'. Those grand words hid the reality that cheating would always form part of such a brutal and demanding event – and indeed it still does to this day. Desgrange, however, wanted to rescue his race from the mob and gentrify it, to turn it into a sporting competition of real worth. That led to better organization and shorter stages, as well as stricter rules and the inclusion of the mountain passes. In this way the structure of the modern Tour was born.

The first mountain climb, the Ballon d'Alsace, appeared on the route in 1905. On that first ascent, René Pottier was the only competitor able to ride all the way to the summit, but Desgrange's imagination was nonetheless fired by the epic scale and potential drama of the high passes. By 1910 Desgrange took the race into the wilderness of the bear-inhabited and snowbound Pyrénées, and in a particularly brutal stage, which has since passed into Tour folklore, the riders tackled four passes – the Peyresourde, Aspin, Tourmalet and Aubisque. Octave Lapize won that first pioneering haul, only to be killed during the First World War when flying as a fighter pilot.

A year later Desgrange went a step further and added the monstrous Alpine climb of the Col du Galibier, north of Briançon. The terrifying mountain passes, he had realized, were at the heart of the blossoming appeal of the Tour. But Desgrange was indifferent to the pain such daunting stages inflicted on the riders. Instead, he spoke in florid French of 'a common celebration of the divine bicycle, the first successful effort of intelligent life to triumph over the laws of weight'. Such extravagance spawned a literary tradition centred on the Tour's heroic values that many still subscribe to. Even today, the press corps awards an annual prize for the best feature story written during the Tour – but only if written in French.

To some, Desgrange was a poetic visionary, to others a tyrannical obsessive, but he was far from alone in his fascination for the race. In 1912 the French novelist Colette, working as a correspondent for *Le*

Matin, watched the race pass, noting in awe that 'the riders were the only quiet people in all the uproar; their silence seemed to cut them off from what was happening all round them'. Even today, Colette would have much the same impression, of entranced athletes, cocooned within the bubble of the race.

As the Tour developed, the mountains increasingly held sway and the Alps and the Pyrénées became fixtures on the route. In 1913 came the moment seen by many as the encapsulation of the Tour's capacity for near-comical cruelty. As the race traversed the Pyrénées, Eugène Christophe was leading the field when his bicycle frame snapped on the long and rocky descent of the Col du Tourmalet. Back then, there were no support cars handily placed to supply a spare bike and, anyway, Desgrange, in typically lenient style, had banned all outside assistance. So, faced with little other choice, Christophe put his bike on his shoulder and continued the rough descent on foot. He walked 14 kilometres and saw most of his rivals sweep past, the time so painfully gained on the ascent of the giant Tourmalet ebbing away. Finally, he came to a blacksmith's forge in Sainte-Marie-de-Campan and, although exhausted, began to painstakingly weld together his snapped bicycle, using the most basic tools. Watched by race officials, Christophe was aided by a small boy who worked the forge bellows as he repaired the frame of his bike. But that slight assistance, even after everything else he'd been through, was against the rules. The draconian Desgrange slapped a time penalty on him to add to the four hours he had already lost, his cruelty unwittingly ensuring Christophe's place in Tour legend.

There are echoes of that resilience to be found in the modern Tour, although the increasingly globalized race sometimes struggles to retain the integral hardships exemplified by Christophe's tale. Even so, Lance Armstrong, the former cancer-sufferer who has dominated the Tour since 1999, admits that he taps into his experience of the pain of chemotherapy to survive the hardest moments of the race. The Texan says that enduring and subsequently surviving cancer gave him the characteristics necessary to become a Tour champion. The uncompromising Armstrong may have little time for the niceties of French cultural history or the Tour's genteel traditions, but in terms of developing the race's global appeal his four emphatic wins have been a resounding marketing success. Not that Desgrange would have much time for a rider who barely speaks French, rides conservatively for most of the season and who once observed, a little dismissively, that 'the Tour is a bike race – not a popularity contest'.

In fact, Desgrange might well be bemused by the international character of the modern Tour and by the globalization that has led to a television audience of two billion people in 165 different countries. Women, banned from the event in his day, now work among the press corps and for the teams and the race organization; English, rather than French, is increasingly the common language used by both the media and the riders; but hardest of all to bear would be the realization that success in his beloved race has become the domain of foreigners. A Frenchman, Bernard Hinault, last won in 1985 and in the Tour's centenary year there is no credible domestic challenger emerging from the peloton, ready to end the Armstrong Era.

Since Greg LeMond's ground-breaking victory in 1986, when the American resisted French favourite Hinault to become the first English-speaking winner of the Tour, the home nation has fallen by the wayside. LeMond's two subsequent successes, in 1989 and 1990, both of which came after he nearly died in a shooting accident, only hastened the decline of French cycling. Since then, a Spaniard, a Dane, a German, an Italian and Armstrong have claimed the Tour's yellow jersey, and none of them were even riding for a French sponsor. As the Tour rolls through the French countryside, the home nation's riders have become strangers in their own land.

Yet as the doping scandals of 1998 revealed, some things haven't changed. Cheating still goes on, although Desgrange might not recognize its more sophisticated and subtle forms. With sabotage no longer an option, hi-tech doping has increasingly become a problem. Genetic manipulation, human growth hormones and blood enhancement therapies are all now part of the drug pharmacopeia that shadows professional cycling. Remarkably, the first drugs tests weren't introduced until 1968 and that was largely as a result of British rider Tom Simpson's demise in the broiling heat of Mont Ventoux the previous July. Unsurprisingly, the riders objected to the first tests and there were protests, strikes and go-slows. But the days of the most blatant acts of deception were effectively ended by the Tour's growing popularity around the world. With television cameras at every turn, it has become much harder to cheat and, in fact, the quality and credibility of the race as a spectacle has been greatly improved by the tighter controls.

Despite the controversies and the commercialism, the modern Tour is still as touched with romance, poignancy and heroism as Desgrange's inaugural race in 1903. It is wholly in keeping with the Tour's remarkable history that for the past four years a maverick Texan, his resolve to endure hardened by appalling suffering, has ridden through the dappled sunshine of the Parisian afternoon to victory.

1900s

It cost just 10 French francs to enter the first Tour de France, which left the Café 'Le Réveil Matin' in Montgeron, in the suburbs of Paris, at 16 minutes past 3 in the afternoon of July 1, 1903. The 2,428 kilometre route was split into 6 stages, with rest days between each gargantuan leg of the race.

Of 60 starters, only 21 reached the Parc des Princes in Paris, where, on July 19, diminutive chimney sweep Maurice Garin became the first Tour de France champion, winning by 2 hours 49 minutes. The last rider in the race, or *lanterne rouge*, finished 64 hours, 47 minutes, 22 seconds behind him. Garin's victory in the inaugural event ensured he was seen as a pioneer, much like the other explorers and adventurers of the early 20th century.

Born a French-speaking Italian in the Aosta valley in 1871, Garin grew up travelling around Europe and had become accustomed to life on the road. Already an accomplished racer, he started that first Tour as a favourite, and won the 467 kilometre opening stage from Paris to Lyon. In 1904 he was again favourite and won for a second time, but when race director Henri Desgrange found himself swamped by allegations of cheating, Garin and the next three finishers were among those disqualified and Henri Cornet was announced as Tour champion. Bitterly disappointed, Garin opened a garage in Lille and never came to the Tour again.

By 1905, when the race moved to a points classification, Desgrange, stung by the controversies, was calling the Tour the 'great cycling crusade', a sentiment echoed by current race director Jean-Marie Leblanc after similar scandals overwhelmed the Tour in 1998. Louis Trousselier won in 1905, as the Vosges and the Alps made their debut, but there were more incidents of sabotage – on the final stage all the riders, except one, suffered punctures, as nails were scattered on the road.

As the mountain stages became more prominent, René Pottier was rewarded with victory in 1906, when he mastered the Ballon d'Alsace, the Côte de Laffrey and the Col Bayard. Three riders were thrown off the race in Dijon for catching a train, but that didn't prevent Pottier, winner of four consecutive mountain stages, from securing an emphatic win.

Lucien Petit-Breton, who famously slept with his bike in his bedroom, was born in Brittany but had lived in South America, where he had worked as a bellhop at the Buenos Aires Jockey Club. Petit-Breton took fourth place in the 1906 Tour, but in 1907 decisively took the race lead four stages from Paris. He won again in 1908 but opted to retire to the Périgord region, only to miss racing so badly that he reversed his decision. Five years later, in 1913, he might have won a third Tour, but for a heavy fall that forced him to quit the race.

The Tour's first decade ended with the first non-French victory: François Faber of Luxembourg won the 1909 Tour in appalling weather, winning six stages, including the leg to Belfort following a 255 kilometre breakaway in a snowstorm.

Left: Maurice Garin, the 32-year-old chimney sweep who won the first Tour de France in 1903. The first prize was 3,000 francs. Garin crossed the line first again in 1904 – but was later disqualified, along with the next three riders, for covering part of a stage on a train.

Opposite: Garin, his brother César and their French team-mate Lucien Pothier enjoy a drink with supporters, 1904.

Opposite: Lucien Petit-Breton, winner of the 1907 and 1908 Tours, at the Parc des Princes, Paris. 'Petit-Breton' – the name he was always known by, even officially – was in fact a nickname, his real surname being Mazan. He was also nicknamed 'The Argentine', since he was brought up in Argentina.

Right: René Pottier, the winner of the 1906 Tour, seen here with his wife, did not live to defend his title. He committed suicide the following January, aged just 29.

Above: Maurice Garin (second rider from left) prepares for his lap of honour at Paris' Parc des Princes, 1903.

Left: Picking up tacks and nails from the road at the Boc Aquaduct, 1904. Sabotage was a big feature of the early Tours – the following year over 200 pounds of nails were found on the opening stage.

Opposite: Horseplay in the 1908 Tour between Lucien Petit-Breton (left) and Georges Passerieu.

Opposite, top: The Alcyon team that won the Tour in 1909, with Luxembourg's François Faber – the Tour's first non-French champion – second left. Faber won five consecutive stages – but not the longest, the epic 413 kilometre 13th stage run from Brest to Caen.

Opposite, bottom: Emile Georget and Lucien Petit-Breton, 1907. Georget had led the race until well over half way, only to be docked a decisive number of points for changing bicycles during a stage, which was banned under the Tour's strict rules.

Below: Georges Passerieu and Lucien Petit-Breton on their way back to their hotel, during the 1908 Tour.

Above: Lucien Petit-Breton (left) and Jean-Baptiste Dortignacq at the Parc des Princes velodrome in Paris, 1905.

Opposite: Aftermath of a crash on a remote road in the 1908 race: Tour founder Henri Desgrange (centre) inspects Georges Passerieu's bike – while Albert Dupont takes the chance to clean up.

Opposite: Jean-Baptiste Dortignacq at the 1905 Tour, where he won three stages and finished third overall.

Right: Count von Zeppelin (left) with Louis Trousselier, the 1905 Tour champion, in 1907. Like many of his contemporaries, Trousselier took a win-at-all-costs approach to the Tour: in 1905 he had taken to smashing the inkstands at checkpoints en route, to delay the riders behind him.

Below: François Faber, the 1909 Tour champion.

On the road to Lunéville, during the 1908 Bayonne–Bordeaux stage.

Above: Riders during the Bayonne–Bordeaux stage, 1908. The Tour has visited Bordeaux more times than any other town or city – apart from Paris.

Opposite: Negotiating the cobbles in Lille towards the end of the first stage of the 1906 Tour. The riders' day had begun in Paris at 5a.m. Typically, start times in the early years of the Tour were between midnight and 6a.m., to allow the 300–400 kilometre stages to be completed in daylight the following afternoon.

René Pottier on his way to victory in 1906.

Lucien Petit-Breton and François Faber – who would finish first and second on the
podium – lead the peloton in Rouen, 1908.

Above: René Pottier leads the way through a village on the Bordeaux–Nantes stage, 1906.

Right: Riders recuperate with beer and a song at Bayonne, 1909.

1910s

In truth, the Tour de France was still in its infancy as it entered its second decade, the years that witnessed the Great War, the sinking of the Titanic and Henri Desgrange's tyrannical and infamous decision to penalize Eugène Christophe for accepting help when repairing his bike in a blacksmith's forge in the Pyrénées.

Desgrange became sick in the July of 1910 and had to leave the race at Luchon. He delegated his powers to Victor Breyer, who watched the curly-haired Octave Lapize overwhelm François Faber of Luxembourg in the mountains, as the Pyrénées, reconnoitred in a snowstorm prior to the race by Alphonse Steines, made their debut. Showing a surprisingly humane side to his character, Desgrange also instigated the *voiture-balai*, or broom wagon, a van to pick up those who were too exhausted to continue the race. Others, however, said that this was simply a canny measure to prevent the more extreme cases of cheating at the back of the race.

Gustave Garrigou won in 1911, when only 28 riders completed a 5,343 kilometre route that took in the Télégraphe, Galibier and Allos climbs in the Alps and included 14 rest days. These were heady days: Desgrange published his poem of 'Adoration', eulogizing the mysterious appeal of the Alps and Pyrénées, riders such as Garrigou began to experiment with gear ratios for the mountain stages and there was the tale of Paul Duboc, poisoned during the race, but who still managed to win four stages and finish second overall.

The slightly shorter 1912 race saw Odile Defraye become the Tour's first Belgian champion, after his Alcyon trade team gave him strong support throughout the race, frustrating Eugène Christophe's best efforts. The Frenchman dominated the Alpine stages, memorably winning in Grenoble after crossing the Galibier summit alone, during an epic 315 kilometre breakaway.

Defraye's victory had opened the door to Belgian riders and in 1913, as the race abandoned the points system and readopted the time classifications still used today, Philippe Thys took the first of his three wins, an achievement that would not be matched until Louison Bobet equalled it 40 years later. Thys, in only his second professional season, fought out a gripping duel with Lucien Petit-Breton, that ended only when the French rider crashed out of the Tour, after fracturing his kneecap, on the penultimate day.

The 1914 Tour took place under the shadow of impending war between France and Germany, and the race ended in Paris just one week before hostilities began. Thys' second victory came only after he was put under immense pressure, first by the unlikely Oscar Egg and later by the determined Henri Pelissier, who battled against Thys until the very last day and lost the race to the resilient Belgian by just 1 minute and 50 seconds.

In June 1919, Desgrange took the Tour back on the road seven months after the Armistice was declared, the war years having claimed three former champions – François Faber, Octave Lapize and Lucien Petit-Breton. In the year that first saw the introduction of the race leader's easily distinguished yellow jersey, or *maillot jaune*, Firmin Lambot continued the line of Belgian success, but the decade will always be remembered for the tale of Eugène Christophe and his calvary on the Col du Tourmalet.

Left: Octave Lapize was to be the 1910 Tour champion, but found the mountains, especially the newly included Pyrénéan peak, the Tourmalet, heavy-going. Riding conditions on the Tourmalet were extreme enough for the whole venture to be seen by many observers as one of Tour organizer Henri Desgrange's publicity stunts. Lapize emerged on the other side of the climb, with one choice word for the waiting Tour officials: 'Assassins'. The 1910 race did see the Tour's first fatality, though the harsh conditions were not to blame: Adolphe Hélière was bathing in Nice on the rest day, when he was stung by a jellyfish. Lapize himself was to die in airborne combat in the First World War.

Opposite: Eugène Christophe passes Emile Engel on the Galibier in 1913. After the war, Christophe would become the first rider to wear the leader's yellow jersey, when it was introduced in 1919.

Lucien Petit-Breton, riding in his eighth Tour, 1913. He was to die in the First World War, along with fellow Tour winners Octave Lapize and François Faber.

Opposite: Eugène Christophe in the mountains, 1912. Christophe became one of the Tour legends, riding the race first in 1906 and for the last time in 1925, when he was 40.

Right: Christophe in 1913, the year he became one of the unluckiest riders in Tour history. When the forks of his bike broke in the Pyrénées, Christophe walked 14 kilometres down the mountain to repair them himself on an anvil in a village forge – but, having a young boy operate the bellows was adjudged to be using outside help and Christophe was given a time penalty on top of the four hours he had already lost. The 326 kilometre stage took him 17 hours 44 minutes to complete (the Swiss rider Celidonio Morini took an incredible 21 hours 24 minutes).

Gustave Garrigou in 1914, when he finished fifth. The Frenchman was one of the leading lights of the Tour's first decade, finishing on the podium six times between 1907 and 1913, and winning the title in 1911.

1920s

As the 1920s began, Belgian cycling was the dominant force in the Tour de France, a succession of victories leading in 1920 to Philippe Thys' third win. Born in 1890 in Anderlecht, Thys was a steady, solid rider, whose penchant for long-distance racing was ideally suited to the Tour. He was unspectacular but effective, which might explain his nickname, 'The Basset Hound'.

The 1920 Tour, in which Belgian riders won 12 stages, was also characterized by the heroic performance of Honoré Barthélémy, who finished eighth despite a series of crashes that fractured his shoulder and wrist. Barthélémy's sufferance was seen in contrast to Henri Pelissier's tantrum over a time penalty, which led him to quit the race. 'He doesn't know how to suffer,' wrote Henri Desgrange dismissively. 'He'll never win the Tour.'

Belgium won again through Léon Scieur in 1921 and then Firmin Lambot in 1922, a year which saw Eugène Christophe wear the yellow jersey at 37 years of age; but it was Henri Pelissier, so close to victory in 1914 and written off by Desgrange in 1920, who finally won in 1923. Pelissier had already nominated his successor as Tour champion. 'Bottecchia will succeed me,' he said of the young Italian stonemason who finished second to him in 1923. Pelissier was right; Ottavio Bottecchia wore the yellow jersey in Paris for the next two years, bringing Italy its first Tour de France champion.

But while Bottecchia was enjoying his success, the relationship between Pelissier, his two brothers and race director Desgrange had reached a new low, after Henri stormed out of the 1924 Tour, following yet another draconian ruling by the authoritarian Desgrange. Pelissier's rage, in the Café de la Gare at Coutances, against the cruel conditions of racing was documented by journalist Albert Londres, who famously wrote a story for the *Petit Parisien* entitled 'The Convicts of the Road'. Pelissier, always an impatient and volatile man, was killed by his mistress in 1935, in a crime of passion.

The circumstances surrounding Bottecchia's premature death, at the age of 30, continue to fascinate to this day. In June 1927 he was found unconscious in a vineyard near his home in Italy, with serious head wounds. Twenty years later a farmer confessed on his deathbed to having hurled rocks at a cyclist who was picking grapes on his land, but others have suggested that Bottecchia's liberal leanings had led him to be brutally beaten by Italian neo-fascists.

Belgian Lucien Buysse took his only Tour win in 1926, prior to Luxembourger Nicolas Frantz's double wins of 1927 and 1928 and a further Belgian success from Maurice Dewaele in 1929. Frantz's victories were both accomplished, but in 1928 his second win was threatened by a bizarre mechanical incident, three days from Paris, as he comfortably led the race. On the road to Charleville, his bike fell apart on a railway crossing. A spare machine could not be found and Frantz was forced to use a woman's commuting bike, with mudguards and lights attached. Frantz picked up speed again and, at an average of 27 kilometres an hour, arrived at the finish 28 minutes behind his rivals. Yet the lead he had amassed over the course of the race was such that he still won that year's Tour by more than 50 minutes.

Guillaume Cecherelli on the Galibier
during the epic Grenoble–Gex stage
of 1920. The 362 kilometre run saw the
final group finish nearly three hours
behind the winner.

Left: Noel Amenc gets off and pushes on the Pyrénéan stage to Luchon, 1920.

Opposite: Crowds invade the Parc des Princes velodrome, after Philippe Thys' victory in the 1920 race is confirmed. The remaining riders had to finish the race on foot.

Above: Benjamin Jamaux comes to grief at Guignes, 1921.

Opposite: Jamaux at the finish of the 12th stage in Strasbourg, later in the 1921 Tour. His bike had been damaged beyond use en route from Geneva and the Belgian had ended up having to carry it the rest of the way, in accordance with Tour rules, which still forbade outside assistance or the use of replacement bikes.

Opposite and right: Ottavio Bottecchia, the first Italian winner of the Tour, 1924. He led the race from start to finish, and won again the following year. He was killed in mysterious circumstances in 1927 while out on a training ride. The mystery remains unsolved, though some believe that he had incurred the wrath of Italian fascists.

Below: Belgium's Philippe Thys, winner in 1913, 1914 and 1920 – the first rider to win the Tour three times.

Left: Firmin Lambot – Tour champion in 1919 and 1922 – and Joseph Muller fill up with water.

Above: Philippe Thys on the way to Grenoble, 1920.

Double stage winner Robert Jacquinot
stops for soup in Hostens, 1922.

Above: Hector Uberghen gets a tow from a fan, 1924.

Opposite: Ottavio Bottecchia takes the dusty way to victory, 1924.

The peloton on the Col d'Allos during
the Nice–Briançon stage, 1924.

Charlie Chaplin keeps watch over spectators between Le Havre and Cherbourg, 1925.

Above: Italy's Michele Gordini in the Pyrénées, 1927. At one point of this 326 kilometre stage from Bayonne to Luchon, he was nearly an hour ahead of the field – only for technical problems to relegate him to fifth by the end.

Opposite: Belgium's Louis Muller and Luxembourg's Nicolas Frantz – the yellow jersey and eventual overall winner – on the penultimate stage of the 1927 race, from Charleville to Dunkerque.

Luxembourg's Nicolas Frantz leads the
Tour from Briançon to Evian, 1927. Franz
would go on to win the race overall, and
again in 1928.

1930s

In the wake of the sponsor Alcyon's monopoly on success in the late 1920s, race director Henri Desgrange radically changed the formula of the Tour in 1930, and created a race based on eight elite national teams, with France well represented by additional regional teams. But Desgrange had become such a puritan that, additionally, he decided to provide anonymous unbranded bikes for the riders, rather than support trade names. He also created the publicity caravan of sponsored vehicles, which covered a substantial part of the spiralling costs of staging the Tour.

Frenchman André Leducq may not have been the best climber in that year's race, but he was a daredevil descender, always capable of making up for lost time. Sometimes, though, he took a risk too far and in 1930 fell twice on the descent of the Col du Galibier, injuring his knee, while wearing the yellow jersey. Incredibly, the whole of the French national team waited to pace Leducq up to the field again, even though he was the best part of 15 minutes behind. Even more remarkably, Leducq then won the stage and went on to victory in Paris.

Antonin Magne, who in later years became team manager to Louison Bobet and Raymond Poulidor, took his first Tour victory in 1931, after expertly preparing for the key stage in the Pyrénées, between Pau and Luchon. Magne spent four weeks training on the mountain passes, a strict regime that might even have put the meticulous Lance Armstrong to shame.

In 1932 Leducq won again, taking 5 stage wins and wearing the yellow jersey for 18 days. The success of the French national team continued and the victory of Georges Speicher in 1933 was followed by Magne's second win in 1934. That year's Tour is remembered for the sacrifice of René Vietto, who tearfully forsook his hopes of victory by giving Magne his own wheel after the race leader had crashed in the Pyrénées.

Belgium's Romain Maes ended the French hegemony in 1935, leading from start to finish in a dramatic Tour marred by the death in the Alps of Spain's Francesco Cepeda. Appropriately, Maes won both the first stage, in Lille, and the last, in Paris. But his achievement was surpassed by that of Sylvère Maes, who won utterly convincingly in both 1936 and 1939. Maes, from Flanders in Belgium, was a powerful rather than stylish rider, but that didn't prevent him from beating Magne by more than 25 minutes in 1936 and Vietto by over 30 minutes three years later.

The French national team won again, through Roger Lapébie, in 1937, after a scandal over an illegal alliance between Flemish riders saw defending champion Sylvère Maes quit the race in Bordeaux. But Lapébie was further assisted by the fate of Italian hero Gino Bartali, who crashed into a riverbed and abandoned the Tour, 24 hours after he had thrashed the field on the slopes of the Galibier.

The Italian was crowned as the new *campionissimo* in 1938, after a phenomenal breakaway in the high Alps secured victory. 'Don't touch him, he is a god,' shouted the President of the Italian Cycling Federation when fans gathered around Bartali. But their elation was short-lived as the arrival of the Second World War, so it seemed, threatened to rob Bartali of the prospect of any further Tour wins.

Opposite: André Leducq, winner in 1930. Note the spare tyre slung over his shoulder, a common sight in the early decades of the Tour. Leducq was the first French winner for seven years, his triumph coming in a race that had been drastically revamped: riders rode for national teams, rather than manufacturers' and rode identical bikes. This was also the first year of the publicity caravan, a big parade of sponsors' floats and novelties that preceded the cyclists along the Tour route – and helped pay for the race.

Above: Oscar Thierbach struggles in the mud on the Col du Tourmalet, 1931.

Legendary exotic dancer Josephine Baker was the celebrity starter for the 1933 Tour.

Above: Only 4,470 kilometres to go: the peloton at the start in Paris, 1934.

Opposite: Eventual winner Antonin Magne remounts on the Col d'Aubisque, 1934. This was Magne's second victory, after his success in 1931.

Opposite: Yellow jersey Romain Maes meets the World's Strongest Man, Charles Rigoulet, 1935.

Above: Maes reunited with his mother after his Tour win, 1935.

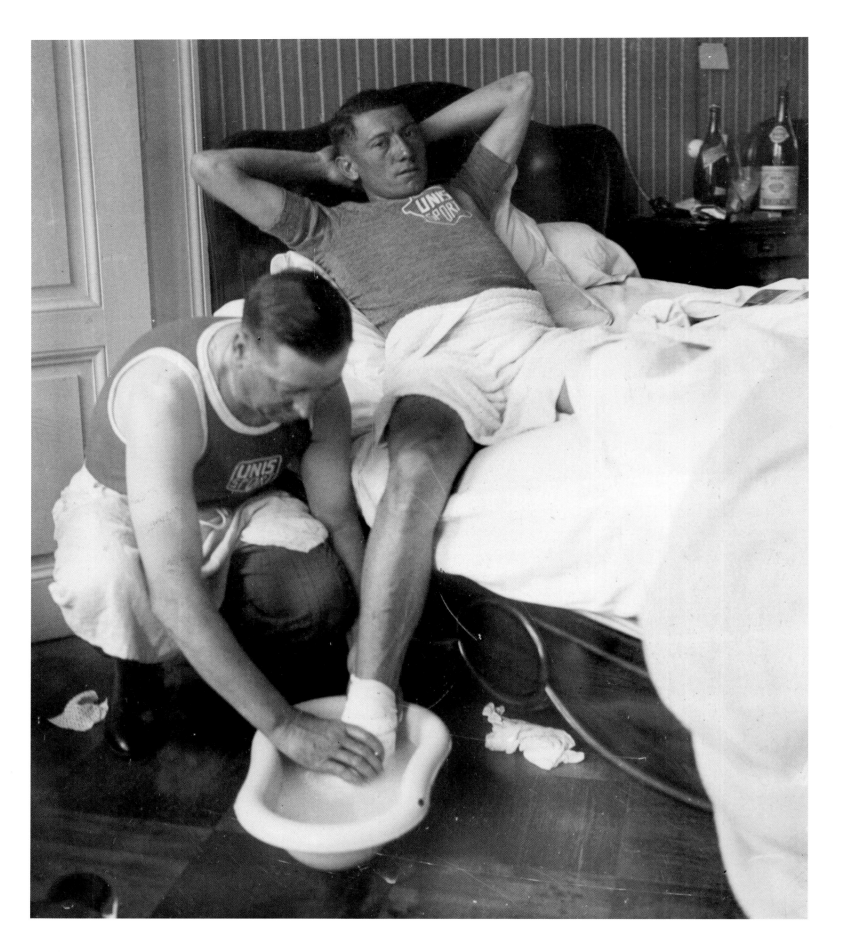

Opposite: Fernand Mithouard seeks reinvigoration, 1936.

Above: Jean Aerts and Romain Maes answer questions from young fans, 1935.

Right: Italian riders play snooker on the Tour rest day in Pau, 1935.

The 1937 champion Roger Lapébie leads the peloton across a level crossing.

Above: Before the time trial: Francesco Lamusso and Roger Lapébie, 1937.

Opposite: Eloi Meulenberg meets the fans before the stage start in Narbonne, 1937.

Left: Gino Bartali alone on the
Col d'Izoard, 1938, on his way to overall
victory. The Italian would win the race
again a decade later.

Above: Bartali salutes the crowd at the
Parc des Princes, Paris, 1938.

Crossing the Pont de St André
at Cubzac, in Bordeaux, 1938.

Above: Antonin Magne heads the lead group across the l'Oise, 1938.

Opposite: Hijinks on the 1938 Tour.

René Vietto (left), in the yellow jersey and team-mate Oreste Bernardoni on the Col d'Izoard in 1939. Vietto had been leading the race for nearly two weeks only to lose 20 minutes on this, the 15th stage. Belgium's Sylvère Maes won the stage and went on to win the race.

1940s

War in Europe interrupted the Tour between 1939 and 1947, and with France under German occupation professional racing on such a grand scale was impossible. The Tour's founder, Henri Desgrange, died in 1940, but new race director Jacques Goddet was just as much a traditionalist as his predecessor. When the racing resumed in 1947 there were few significant changes, other than the introduction of two wild and remote Alpine passes, the Col du Glandon and the Col de la Croix de Fer.

The first post-war Tour fell to Jean Robic of the West France regional team, but only after René Vietto, a former bellhop who had twice worn the yellow jersey, lost the lead in a time trial to Pierre Brambilla, 48 hours from the finish in Paris. Robic, who before leaving for the race had promised his wife that he would win first prize, rode brilliantly in the Pyrénées and had the last word, clinching what was an unexpected victory on the final stage to the Parc des Princes.

To some minds, Vietto's career was more notable for his bizarre efforts to minimize his racing weight, than for his competitive achievements. The Frenchman was fascinated by innovations and, as an accomplished climber, obsessed with reducing his load in the mountain passes. So concerned, in fact, that he had a toe amputated.

By 1948 the religious Gino Bartali, who had first won the Tour ten years earlier, was the darling of the Italian fans, the *tifosi*. 'Gino the Pious' was untouchable in that year's race, winning seven stages and the 'King of the Mountains' prize. But the ageing Bartali was about to face a new challenge from within his own team when, in 1949, the brilliant but ultimately tragic Fausto Coppi revealed the range of his abilities with his first Tour win. Tensions between Coppi and Bartali had been resolved only two weeks before the start of the race when, at a meeting in Chiavari, Italy, Italian team coach Alfredo Binda eased the Italian rivals into a collaborative pact that dominated that year's Tour. With two time trial wins and an unstoppable ride through the Alps, which won him the 'King of the Mountains' classification, Coppi took final victory in Paris, with a 10-minute lead over Bartali.

Yet Coppi's was an unfulfilled talent. He had survived active service in the Second World War, including two years spent in a prisoner of war camp, a sex scandal and the rivalry of the Italian national team, only to be killed by malarial pneumonia in January 1960, aged 40. In the post-war period, Coppi's elegance and his public extra-marital affair with 'the White Lady' became a symbol of inspiration for liberal Italy. His freedom of spirit shone through when he was racing and many regard him as the greatest natural talent the Tour has ever seen.

Left: The peloton climbs the Col du Glandon, on the stage from Grenoble to Briançon, 1947.

Above: Spectators help Gino Bartali remount in 1948. The Italian went on to win his second Tour title ten years after his first.

Above: Louison Bobet and Gino Bartali on the road to the summit of the Col de la Croix de Fer, 1947.

Opposite: Gino Bartali on the Croix de Fer on the same stage in 1948.

The waiting game: spectators picnic away the last hours before the arrival of the Tour for the first time in eight years, 1947.

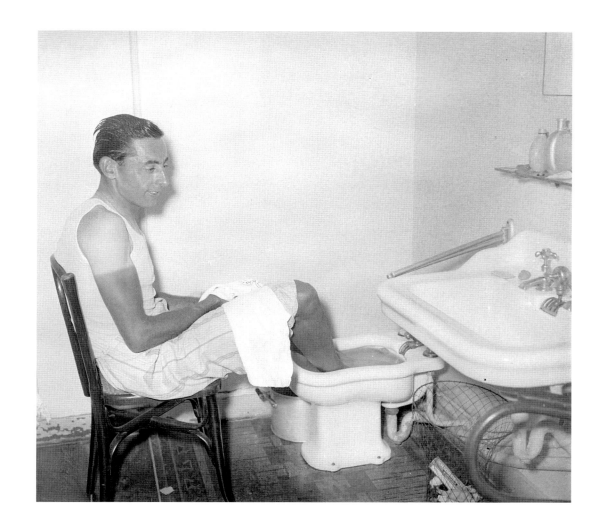

Left: Stopping for refreshments on the stage from Brussels to Luxembourg, 1947.

Above: Fausto Coppi was 29 when he rode his first Tour de France in 1948. By then, the Italian many still believe to be the greatest rider ever had already won the Tour of Italy at his first attempt (aged 20) and spent two years in British prisoner-of-war camps. He was to win two Tours, in 1949 and 1952.

Jean Robic, 1947 Tour winner, crosses the summit of the Col du Tourmalet, over four minutes ahead of the peloton. Robic's stage win clawed him back towards overall contention – and he was to clinch victory on the last day of the race in Paris, without having worn the race leader's jersey.

Below: Dancing the hours away waiting for the peloton, 1947.

Right: Riders stock up on wine on the Brussels–Luxembourg stage, 1947.

Above: Louison Bobet meets Monsignor Théas, hero of the French Resistance, 1948.

Opposite: Gino Bartali arrives for the 1948 Tour, with fans and entourage.

Above: Jean Robic gets a soaking, 1947.

Opposite: Fausto Coppi and Gino Bartali, the two greatest riders of the day, in the Alps, 1949. Italian fans divided on regional lines in their support for the pair: Coppi, the ahead-of-his-time professional, steeped in new ideas of training, diet and performance enhancement, was the hero of the urban north of the country; Bartali, whose greatest support was his deep religious faith, the hero of the rural south. The cultural divide between the two became all the greater in the 1950s, after Coppi left his wife to live with his mistress.

1950s

If any era is seen as cycling's Golden Age it is the 1950s. Since 1930 the Tour's structure had been based around national teams, forcing riders who spent most of the year riding for rival sponsors to unite under their national colours. Within the Italian and French teams, in particular, this was a blueprint for the most bitter infighting and division during the post-war years.

As the decade began the search for fresh terrain led to the opening up of new mountain passes – Alpe d'Huez, Mont Ventoux, Puy-de-Dôme and Sestrières – and these new theatres further developed the grandeur and appeal of the event.

In 1950 the volatile Swiss Ferdi Kubler took a win that was credited as much to the absence of Fausto Coppi and the mass withdrawal of the Italians as to his own merits, although that ignores the pressure he faced from Louison Bobet and Raphaël Geminiani of France.

Bobet, a young and intense Breton, began the 1951 Tour as the race favourite, but was overtaken by Swiss Hugo Koblet. Nicknamed the 'Pedaller of Charm', Koblet was credited – in cycling terms at least – with inventing a matinee idol look that became known as the 'Italian Style'. He combined panache with resilience, as exemplified by his 1951 lone stage win in Agen, when he crossed the line ahead of the field, ran a hand through his hair and then stood, calmly checking his stopwatch, while awaiting the finish of his exhausted rivals.

Coppi was back to his best in 1952, winning by almost half an hour and taking all three summit finishes – at Alpe d'Huez, Puy-de-Dôme

and Sestrières – with aplomb. France had now failed to win for five years and Marcel Bidot, new manager of the national team, was determined to arrest the decline.

Without Bidot's canny man-management of his tempestuous riders Bobet might have struggled to win in any year, yet the Breton succeeded in 1953, 1954 and 1955. During that period, he mastered both the mighty Col d'Izoard and, in 1955, the torrid heat of Mont Ventoux.

Fellow Frenchman Roger Walkowiak's win in 1956 was a surprise, but Jacques Anquetil's first win the following year was due to the outstanding supremacy of the French team. He might have won again in 1958, but was forced to abandon because of a pulmonary infection, leaving the door open for the extraordinary Luxembourg rider Charly Gaul. Gaul's performance in 1958 was the stuff of legend. He crushed his rivals on Mont Ventoux, but then lost time due to a mechanical problem. Forty-eight hours later, however, Gaul won in Aix-les-Bains after one of the most inspired solo attacks in Tour history. Gaul's closest rival, Raphaël Geminiani, incensed, turned on his team-mates, yelling at them and accusing them of treason. The French were in danger of ending the decade as they had begun it.

It took a crisis meeting and a pact of sorts to reunite the French for the 1959 Tour, but it was to little avail as Federico Bahamontes, the climber from Spain who would soon become known as the 'Eagle of Toledo', took what was his nation's first-ever overall success in the Tour.

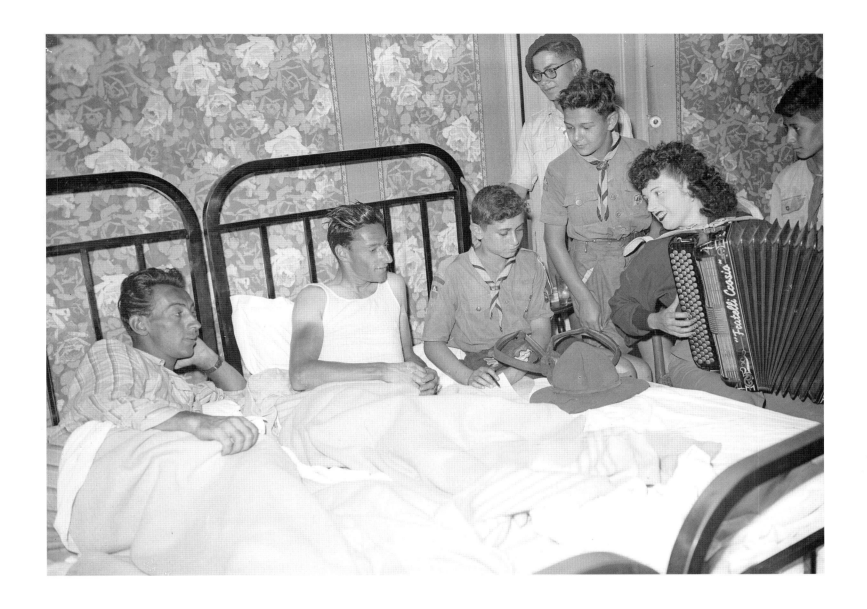

Opposite, top: Orson Welles and the Mayor of Paris get the 1950 race under way.

Opposite, bottom: Legendary French balladeer Charles Trenet enjoys some Gallic clownery with Charly Gaul (left) and Marcel Emzer (right) at a stage start in Toulouse, 1958.

Above: Emilio Croci Forti and Ferdi Kubler have their rest day during the 1951 Tour enlivened by lady accordionist Yvette Horner and a clutch of boy scouts.

Riders cool down in the Mediterranean at St Tropez, 1950.

Opposite: Gino Bartali on his way to complain about his treatment by fans during the 1950 Pyrénéan stage to St Gaudens. He had won the stage, but had been kicked and punched by French spectators during the climb of the Col d'Aspin. Both Italian teams were to withdraw from the race in protest.

Above: Fiorenzo Magni (standing, in pale cardigan) signs autographs after quitting the 1950 Tour. Magni had been in the yellow jersey, when the Italian teams decided to withdraw.

The 1950 Tour champion, Switzerland's
Ferdi Kubler, time trials to victory.

Opposite and above: The dapper Hugo Koblet – punningly known as the 'Pedaller of Charm' – in 1951, when he won the Tour. Known as a laid-back dandy, the Swiss rider carried a comb, a sponge and a small bottle of cologne with him at all times and would pause during the home straight to perfect his grooming, to the delight of fans. After one victory in the 1951 Tour, he also took a long and meaningful look at his watch while waiting for the runner-up to finish. He never finished the Tour again after 1951 – abandoning in 1953 during the tenth stage.

Above: Louison Bobet picks up provisions from French team manager Marcel Bidot at a feed zone, 1953.

Opposite: André Darrigade and fans, 1958. Darrigade took part in every Tour between 1953 and 1966 and finished all of them except one – he also won the green jersey in 1959 and 1961.

Hugo Koblet, three minutes ahead of the peloton, on the bridge at Villeneuve-sur-Lot, 1951.

Above: Fiorenzi Magni, Gino Bartali and Giovanni Corrieri at prayer on the rest day at Lourdes, 1951. Bartali – known as 'Gino the Pious' – was famously devout and enjoyed audiences with Pope Pius XII, who held him up as a spiritual example to Italian youth.

Opposite: Christiane Bobet urges her husband to Tour victory, 1953.

Louison Bobet on his way to the first of three successive wins, in 1953. Note the previous year's winner, Fausto Coppi (in pale shorts), filming a home movie at the roadside.

Above: An exhausted Fausto Coppi at the end of the 16th stage, to Montpellier, 1951. Coppi, still mourning the death of his brother, Serse, just a month previously, finished 33 minutes behind stage winner Hugo Koblet.

Opposite: Italian team manager Alfredo Binda tries to persuade the defeated Coppi not to abandon, 1951.

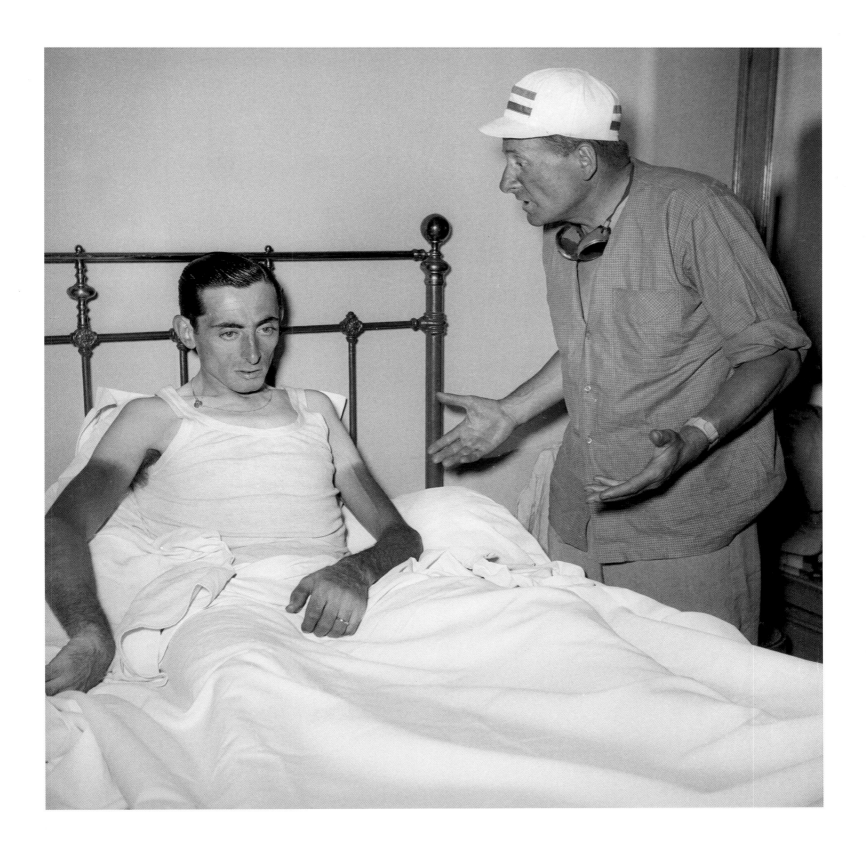

Opposite: Fausto Coppi, *Il Campionissimo*, the 1952 champion.

Right: Wim Van Est clambers back to safety on the Col d'Aubisque in 1951. The first Dutchman ever to wear the yellow jersey, he fell off the road into a ravine and had to be pulled out using the Dutch team's spare inner-tubes threaded together. The tubes were wrecked, and the whole team had to abandon the race as a result.

Remis de ses émotions, Van Est sourit à l'infirmière qui, dans la salle blanche de l'hôpital de Tarbes, lui verse à boire.

Louison Bobet meets his public after his second Tour win, in 1954. The following year, he would become the first rider to win three Tours de France in a row.

The peloton in the Alps, on the
Turin–Grenoble stage, 1956.

Above: The Luxembourg rider Charly Gaul on the Col d'Izoard in 1956.

Right: Gaul rides behind Federico Bahamontes at the summit of the Col du Tourmalet, 1959.

Opposite: Gaul on the barren slopes of Mont Ventoux, 1958, the year he won the Tour.

1958 winner Charly Gaul en route to his famous victory from Briançon to Aix-les-Bains.

1960s

Jacques Anquetil first won the Tour de France in 1957, aged just 24, but came into his own between 1961 and 1964 with a quartet of back-to-back victories. Anquetil's charmed career was in stark contrast to that of fellow Frenchman Raymond Poulidor, who never won the race, despite claiming a top three placing in no fewer than 8 Tours, spanning a period of 14 years. Poulidor, perhaps the greatest Tour rider never to win the race, said that 'the more my popularity grew, the more misery my rivals heaped upon me'. His rivalry with Anquetil divided France, but although in 1964 he lost by only 55 seconds, Poulidor never overcame his more accomplished compatriot.

While 'Pou-pou', as Poulidor was known, won French hearts, Anquetil's economic style and brisk manner won connoisseur's minds. He never set out to be the people's champion, allowing the hapless Poulidor to fulfil that role, but instead married a ruthless efficiency to his pragmatic nature. Yet Anquetil's most famous hour came not in the heat of July, but in June 1965 when, immediately after winning the mountainous Dauphiné Libéré stage race in the Alps, he flew across France, from east to west, and rode in the marathon endurance event from Bordeaux to Paris. It was one of the few occasions in his career when grit won out over panache, as he rode to a memorable victory, despite enduring chronic exhaustion.

Maître Jacques' calculating style won him admirers, but not very many friends, even if away from the races he was something of a *bon viveur*. A taste for seafood, champagne, card schools and drinking contests with Eddy Merckx were hidden behind his aloof public nature. Only after he died of cancer in 1987, at the age of just 54, did the French nation seem able to fully embrace all of his achievements.

After Anquetil's powers had faded came a succession of one-off victories, with Felice Gimondi, Lucien Aimar, Roger Pingeon and Jan Janssen winning between 1965 and 1968. Meanwhile, a youthful Eddy Merckx waited in the wings to initiate the era of domination that began with victory in 1969.

The 1960s also saw the beginning of a new awareness of the dangers of doping. This change in attitude gathered pace after the sickening death, from a cocktail of amphetamines, brandy and heat exhaustion, of Britain's former world champion and genuine Tour contender Tom Simpson, close to the summit of Mont Ventoux. Simpson's death left all those involved in the Tour in a state of shock and a new determination to control the peloton's worst excesses took hold in 1968 with the introduction of medical controls. That resolve to clean things up was hardened in the wake of comments from other leading riders, including Anquetil.

'I don't want to hear the word doping,' he said. 'Rather, one must speak of treatments that are not appropriate for ordinary mortals. You cannot compete in the Tour de France on mineral water alone.'

Opposite and right: Jacques Anquetil won his first Tour de France in 1957 (pictured left) – but it was the early 1960s that saw him dominate the sport. 'Anquetil did for cycling what Mozart did for music,' said his team manager, Raphaël Geminiani. He took consecutive Tour wins from 1961 to 1964 to become the first rider to win the race five times. Regarded as an aloof winning machine by the French public – who warmed more to his oft-beaten rival Raymond Poulidor – Anquetil pioneered his own riding style (the saddle set high, the gears set low) and lived the life of a *bon viveur* even on the Tour – on one stage in 1964 the under-the-weather champ used a water bottle full of champagne to recapture his sparkle.

Above and opposite: Roger Rivière's larks for the press cameras with his wife during the 1960 race were par for the course for a French national hero. The 24-year-old had broken the world hour record three years previously and was on course to win his first Tour. But then disaster struck: descending near Avignon, Rivière came off the road and, on arrival in hospital in Montpellier, it was announced he had broken his back. Rivière later admitted he had been doped so heavily, he had been too weak to pull the brakes. He never regained full use of his limbs.

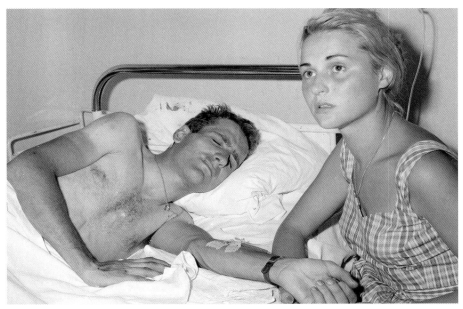

Opposite: The Tour stops to honour President de Gaulle at Colombay-les-Deux-Églises, 1960. The event had been unplanned, but, on learning that the President was at the side of the road, near his residence at Colombay, Tour organizer Jacques Goddet drove through the peloton telling them to stop when they reached the village.

Left: Ireland's Shay Elliott, who led the Tour for three days in 1963.

Below: Local royalty comes out for the Tour, en route to Limoges, 1960.

Jacques Anquetil during the
mountain time trial from Luchon to
Superbagnères, in 1962.

Below: Team manager Raphaël Geminiani gets Anquetil back on the road. Geminiani himself had ridden a then-record 12 Tours – a tally since bettered by a roster of riders led by Holland's Joop Zoetemelk, who finished all 16 times he entered between 1970 and 1986.

Right: Jacques Anquetil and Federico Bahamontes on the Val d'Isère–Chamonix stage, 1963.

Above: Anquetil with his wife, Jeanine, at the Parc des Princes, after clinching his third successive win, 1963.

Opposite: Belgium's Rik Van Looy – winner of two stages in 1965 – accepts the congratulations of a young fan.

Above: Jacques Anquetil reflects on the day's events in Roubaix with TV commentator Robert Chapatte, 1965.

Opposite: Felice Gimondi: the 22-year-old Italian won the Tour in 1965 – he remains the youngest post-Second World War champion.

Above: Jacques Anquetil talks to the press during the abortive Bordeaux–Bayonne stage in 1966. The peloton was walking rather than riding in protest at the Tour organization's attempt to bring in random dope tests.

Opposite: The peloton face stiff competition on the stage to La Rochelle, 1965.

Opposite: Reigning champion Federico Bahamontes heads home to Spain from Dunkerque, after quitting during the first week of the 1960 Tour.

Above: Jan Janssen, the first Dutch rider to win the Tour, 1968.

Opposite: Tom Simpson cultivated the image of an English gentleman for the French press – and became, in 1962, the first English rider to wear the yellow jersey. He rode the Tour seven times in all (and his 1965 World Championship win led to him being voted BBC Sports Personality of the Year), but he was to die tragically, while riding the Tour in 1967.

Left: Simpson climbing Mont Ventoux in 1967. Within minutes he had collapsed at the side of the road – and would later die in hospital.

Below: Simpson's British team-mates Colin Lewis, Barry Hoban and Arthur Metcalfe mourn their friend's death.

Above: Raymond Poulidor, perhaps the greatest Tour rider never to win the race.

Right: Poulidor studies his bloodied nose after a crash in 1968. He finished on the podium eight times, more than any other rider in history, without ever wearing the yellow jersey.

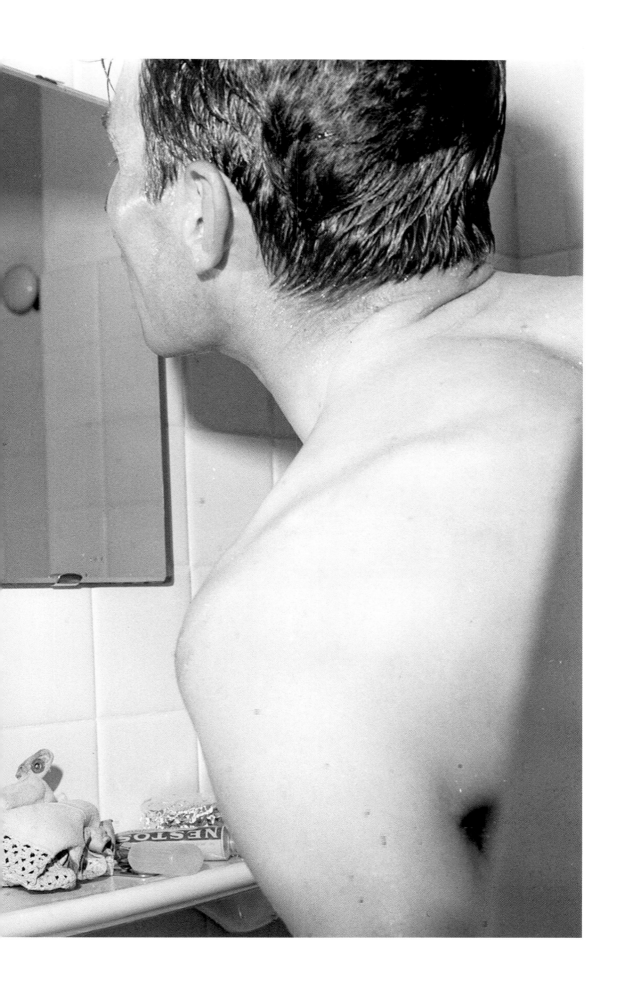

Opposite: Eddy Merckx on the way to his first Tour de France victory in 1969.

Above: The soon to be very familiar sight of Merckx on his lap of honour, at the Parc des Princes, 1969.

1970s

Eddy Merckx, undoubtedly the greatest rider cycling has seen, was the dominant rider of the 1970s, winning five Tours between 1969 and 1974. His insatiable appetite for success earned him the nickname 'The Cannibal' and drove his rivals mad with frustration, because he gave no ground and showed no weakness. Merckx was not happy simply to claim the yellow jersey and win the Tour; he would also fight tooth and nail to win the points classification or the 'King of the Mountains' prize. In 1971 his success rate, against races entered, peaked at an incredible 45 per cent and the rapacious Merckx was seen as cold, ruthless and even inhuman.

Remarkably, his best years in the Tour came after a track racing accident in the autumn of 1969 left him with constant back pain. Merckx overcame this to win 34 Tour stages between 1969 and 1975 and to wear the yellow jersey 96 times. 'He was as hard as nails,' said Roger Swerts, one of his team-mates. 'And we accepted it because that was the way he was with himself.' So resented was the Belgian's domination, however, that riders from rival teams would join forces and turn against him, as happened in the 1972 Giro d'Italia when the Spanish and Italian climbers combined against him. During the 1975 Tour, while climbing the Puy-de-Dôme, he was even punched in the stomach by an embittered French fan.

Through it all, Merckx remained the essence of sporting cool, his brooding good looks ensuring that he had as many adoring fans as he did detractors. He became a sporting icon, to rank with Muhammad Ali, George Best, Jack Nicklaus and Pelé. Merckx was the bridge between the stars of the late 1950s, such as Anquetil and Poulidor, and those who would emerge after his retirement, such as Hinault and LeMond. Even today, he maintains a close relationship with Lance Armstrong and has become a highly influential figure in the American's career.

Merckx was such a dominant champion that the other Tour winners of the decade are often overlooked. He was most threatened by Luis Ocaña of Spain, whose spectacular attacks in the Alpine stages of the 1971 Tour earned him the race lead. But Ocaña crashed heavily in a Pyrénéan thunderstorm and was forced to quit, leaving Merckx to claim another victory, although as a mark of respect to his Spanish rival he refused to wear the yellow jersey the next day. Ocaña's moment finally came in 1973, as he won by more than 15 minutes, although in Merckx's absence his success did not receive the acclaim it perhaps deserved.

It was Frenchman Bernard Thévenet who finally ended the Merckx era, with a spectacular victory in 1975, founded on his performance in the mountain stages. Following Lucien van Impe's win in 1976, Thévenet won again the following year, but in 1978 was himself usurped by a wilful and brilliant 23-year-old from Brittany called Bernard Hinault.

Above and opposite: Belgium's Eddy Merckx, the greatest cyclist that ever lived. He rode an estimated 30,000 miles a year, winning five Tours de France (1969, 1970, 1971, 1972, 1974), and bowed out after the 1977 edition, in which he finished sixth. Merckx did not just build his season around the Tour. 'The Cannibal' raced and won all year round, notching up a total of 525 career wins.

Above: Tour organizer Jacques Goddet lays a wreath on the memorial to Tom Simpson on Mont Ventoux in 1970; the passing Eddy Merckx takes off his cap as a mark of respect.

Opposite: Merckx leads the peloton in the mountains, his great rival, Spain's Luis Ocaña, at his heels, 1972.

Eddy Merckx at the controls during the 1971 Tour.

Above: Spain's Luis Ocaña crashed badly descending the Col de Mente in 1971 – after he fell, three riders hit him, leaving him seriously injured.

Right: Ocaña came back to win the Tour in 1973. He is shown here on the way to victory on stage 8, to Les Orres.

Left: Bernard Thévenet, the 1975 Tour champion, on Mont Ventoux. He was the first French winner for eight years – and would go on to repeat his victory two years later.

Below: Eddy Merckx with Patrick Sercu (left) in 1974. The two men rode as a team in winter track events, but were rivals on the road and at the Tour.

Above: Jean-Pierre Danguillaume and
Bernard Bouffeau making music, 1974.

Opposite: Eddy Merckx seeks divine
assistance during the 1975 Tour.

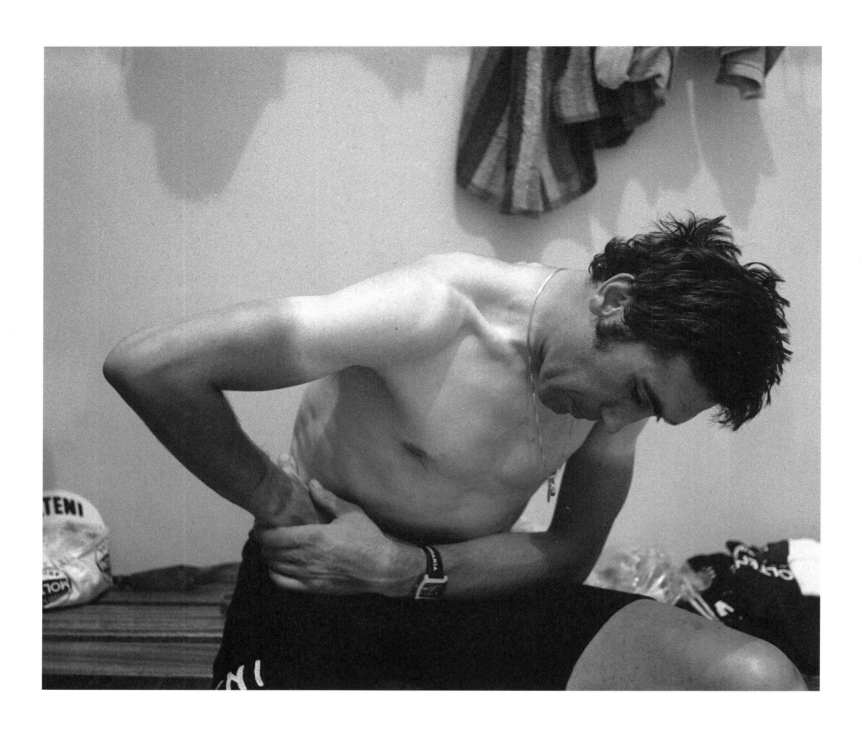

Opposite and above: The almost unstoppable Merckx faced his greatest challenge during the 1975 Tour. First, he was punched in the liver by a roadside spectator. After recovering at the end of the stage (opposite), he identified his attacker to police. Then, he crashed near the start of stage 17, fracturing his cheekbone (above). He still continued to the end of the race – eating only soup – but finished second behind France's Bernard Thévenet.

The Tour came to Britain for a stage in 1974, a less than glamorous day's racing that started and ended in Plymouth, with all the race equipment shipped over by boat.

The last day of the 1975 Tour – the first time the finale took place on the Champs Elysées, rather than the traditional Parc des Princes velodrome.

Above: Stocking up on stage 11,
Montpellier to Argèles-sur-Mer, 1973.

Opposite: The peloton faces the
aftermath of a local protest on the stage
from Nancy to Mulhouse, 1976.

Above: Protesting cattle farmers make their point on the Brive–Clermont-Ferrand stage in 1973.

Opposite: Bernard Hinault leads the riders' strike of 1978. They were protesting about being overworked – with Tour organizers planning more than one stage on some days, racing was sometimes scheduled to start as early as 7.35a.m.

Raymond Poulidor, 40, is presented with
a bust of himself, after completing his last
Tour, in 1976. The veteran French rider
finished third – his eighth podium finish.

Above: Bernard Hinault, third left, in the red, white and blue jersey of the French champion, makes his Tour debut in 1978. Like Jacques Anquetil and Eddy Merckx, he would win the race at his first attempt.

Right: Hinault (left), flanked by his team manager, Cyrille Guimard, realizes he has won back the yellow jersey from Joop Zoetemelk (right) at the end of the Morzine–Avoriaz time trial, 1979.

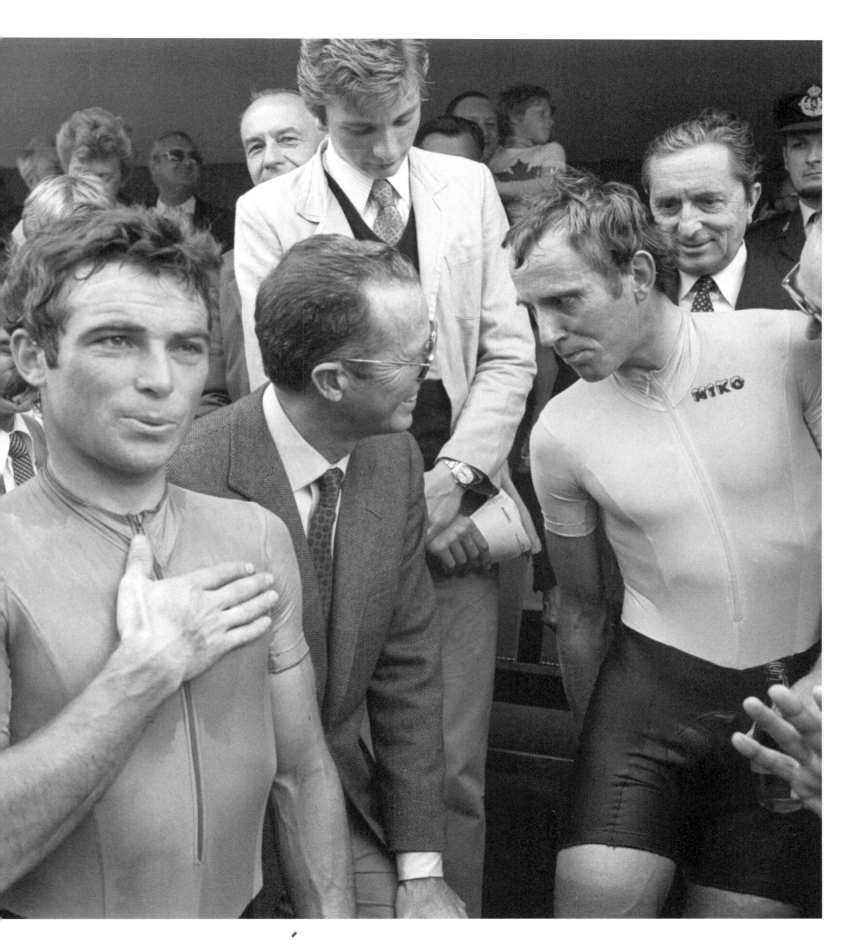

1980s

Two riders, one the epitome of French tradition and the other the embodiment of change, dominated the Tour in the 1980s. Bernard Hinault may have been a farmer's son from Brittany, but he understood the commercial development of cycling. He embraced North American talent, such as Greg LeMond, Andy Hampsten and Steve Bauer, and, realizing that cycling was changing, made allies of them. It was ironic then that he was ultimately usurped by the smart and ambitious LeMond, his protégé from Nevada.

Hinault had been expected to dominate the 1980 Tour, but instead was humiliatingly forced to quit the race, due to a painful knee injury. He slunk out of the race under cover of darkness, in a bid to avoid the scrutiny of the media, but his ploy backfired and he was heavily criticized for his nocturnal exit.

That summer of 1980, as Hinault licked his wounds in Brittany, Dutchman Joop Zoetemelk finally won the Tour at the tenth attempt. But the Breton, stung by his disappointment, was back to his best in 1981 and 1982, winning sprint stages, time trials and mountain stages, with a panache comparable to Eddy Merckx.

In 1983 another knee injury forced him to miss the race altogether. This Tour saw a bespectacled upstart from Paris, Laurent Fignon, steal a shock victory on his debut appearance. Fignon's success was dismissed by many as a fluke, but in 1984, when he toyed with Hinault in the Alps and beat him by more than 10 minutes, that judgement was hastily revised.

The still defiant Hinault was determined to achieve a fifth Tour win, to equal the record set by Merckx and Anquetil. He came to the 1985 Tour with an all-star team that included North Americans LeMond, Hampsten and Bauer and Frenchman Jean-François Bernard. Victory that year took Hinault to his limit. He broke his nose in a crash in St-Etienne and then, suffering from breathing problems, had to tell his understudy LeMond to slow down when the American came close to overthrowing him in the Pyrénées. LeMond checked his pace and let his chance of victory slip away, on the understanding that the favour would be returned.

Predictably, by July 1986 Hinault had forgotten his promise, and the pair became immersed in a bitter spat that split their team into two factions. Living on his nerves, LeMond triumphed and became the Tour's first English-speaking winner, but only after a histrionic Hinault had played mind games so effectively that the American began to suspect his own team personnel of sabotaging his bike. Nearly 20 years later, relations between the pair remain strained.

LeMond's near-fatal hunting accident in 1987 might have overshadowed that year's victory by Dubliner Stephen Roche, had the Irishman not also won the Giro d'Italia and World Championships that season. Roche never again scaled the heights of 1987 but, after Pedro Delgado's success in 1988, LeMond came back to form in 1989 and 1990. In July 1989, the American beat Fignon on the final day by just eight seconds, the narrowest winning margin in the history of the race.

Above: Bernard Hinault during the 1985 Tour – that he would go on to win – with his collection of yellow jerseys. The Frenchman dominated the Tour in the late 1970s and early 1980s, becoming the third rider to win the race five times. His 1985 win remains the last by a French rider – a fact that continues to cause French cycling and the French media increasing anxiety as the 20th anniversary approaches.

Opposite: Hinault during his last appearance at the Tour in 1986. Still in the yellow jersey after the stage to Superbagnères, he finished runner-up to his great rival Greg LeMond in Paris.

Eddy Planckaert (left), Guido Van Calster (middle) and Bernard Hinault neck and neck for the line in a sprint in the 1980 Tour. Note the wet sponges down the riders' backs to keep them cool.

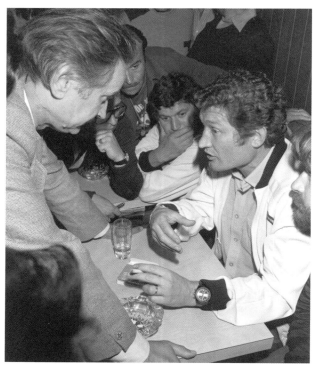

Opposite, top: Hinault leads the peloton over the cobbles on the Lille to Compiègne stage, 1980.

Opposite, bottom: Team manager Cyrille Guimard explains Hinault's mysterious absence to journalists and officials in 1980. In the yellow jersey after stage 12 to Pau, Hinault had been well placed to retain his title – only to quit the race and head for home in the middle of the night, defeated by a long-term knee injury.

Above: Belgium's ace sprinter Freddy Maertens wins the stage from Ireland's Sean Kelly in Nice, 1981.

The peloton, well protected on the
Frankfurt–Metz stage in 1980.

Above: Greg LeMond can only think of the future, as 1985 Tour champion Bernard Hinault shares his delight with Jacques Chirac, then mayor of Paris.

Opposite: LeMond celebrates his win in 1986 – the first-ever by an American rider – with his wife Kathy. Despite being shot in a hunting accident, he would repeat his success in 1989 and 1990.

Opposite: LeMond and Hinault rest up at Alpe-d'Huez, 1986.

Right: Bernard Hinault, French national icon, adds to the legend, 1985.

Below: A rest day massage for Greg LeMond, 1986.

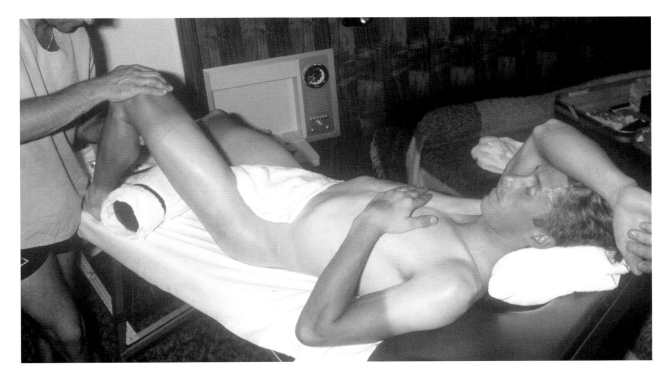

Above: Bernard Hinault leads Greg LeMond over the Col de la Croix de Fer, 1986. Hinault won the stage – but his rival won the race.

Opposite: Luis Herrera before the Tour's start in Berlin, 1987. The Tour started on foreign soil 15 times in its first century, including Brussels (1958), Cologne (1965), Dublin (1998) and Luxembourg (2002).

Left: Goddet still keeping the show on the road, in 1986.

Above: Journalist Jacques Goddet speaking to 1934 champion Antonin Magne. Two years later he became race director, in succession to Henri Desgrange, the Tour founder. Goddet was to run the Tour for over half a century, until 1987.

Left: Tour Feminin champion Jeannie Longo and Tour champion Stephen Roche take their lap of honour, 1987. Roche was the first Irish rider to win the Tour de France.

Below: Roche unwinds after Tour victory, 1987.

Above: A bridge too far? Stage 7, Nantes–l'Ile d'Oléron, 1983.

Opposite: Greg LeMond on his way to a famous victory over local hero Laurent Fignon in Paris, July 1989.

Left and below: A joyful Greg LeMond (left) realizes he has won the 1989 Tour de France, after watching his rival Laurent Fignon (below) finish the last day time-trial. At the start of the day, Fignon – already a two-time Tour winner, in 1983 and 1984 – was in the yellow jersey and set to make it a hat trick. But LeMond, 50 seconds behind overnight, had stormed the 24.5 kilometre course. Fignon, riding last and knowing exactly what he had to achieve, could not hold onto his advantage. LeMond's 8-second margin of victory, after 3,285 kilometres of racing, remains the smallest in Tour history.

1990-
2002

One rider's achievements in the Tour have eclipsed all others over the past decade or so. His first overall victory may not have come until 1999, but Lance Armstrong's very special relationship with the Tour de France actually began in 1993, when, clad in the World Champion's jersey, he took an exuberant stage win in Verdun.

Back then, the feisty Texan was far from the type of durable flyweight blessed with both the patience and the stamina to survive day after day of attrition in the Tour. But his brush with death in 1996, when he was diagnosed with testicular cancer and underwent chemotherapy and brain surgery, changed all that. Armstrong survived and, most crucially, was fired with a new ambition and passion that seemed to sustain him, in the moments when he needed it most. His emergence from his darkest hour coincided with the Tour's search for new life, after the debilitating doping scandals of 1998 had threatened the very existence of the race. Quickly, thanks to both clever marketing and his expansive, inspirational riding style, Armstrong became a superstar and succeeded in popularizing the Tour de France in the United States on a mass scale.

The enormous popularity of Armstrong's four successive wins to date, between 1999 and 2002, have even overshadowed the five consecutive victories of Miguel Indurain, between 1991 and 1995. But then Indurain was a simple man, a quiet and conservative farmer's son from northern Spain. His repeated success was built on a phenomenal time-trialling style.

Sandwiched between the Indurain and Armstrong eras came a trio of opportunists – Bjarne Riis, Jan Ullrich and Marco Pantani – none of whom were more than temporary custodians of the *maillot jaune*. Ullrich, easily the most talented of the three, might well have won more than one Tour, had it not been for Armstrong's resurgence and his own series of traumas, that included weight problems, a drink-driving arrest and a humiliating positive drugs test after an ill-advised visit to a German nightclub.

Pantani, the swashbuckling but erratic climber from Italy who styled himself as 'The Pirate' and rode wearing a bandana and sporting an earring, won the discredited 1998 Tour, only to find himself mired in doping accusations the following summer. Pantani returned to the Tour in 2000 and won two stages, but Armstrong swatted him aside as he rode to the second of his four victories.

The reverberations of the drug scandals of 1998 still continue, but the Société du Tour de France has made a marked effort to clean up the race since then, with a revised ethical code and even stricter testing procedures. In Armstrong, the race found a champion who opened up new territories, and who, just when the race needed it, enhanced the popularity of the Tour around the world. Henri Desgrange would definitely have approved.

Above and opposite: Miguel Indurain (in yellow) dominated the Tour in the early 1990s: the Spaniard was the first rider ever to win five Tours in a row, triumphing every year from 1991–1995. At 1.88 metres, he was the tallest Tour winner in history – and the quiet man from Navarra managed it all while being allergic to dust and pollen …

Opposite: The peloton riding in rural France, 1998.

Above: The Tour fails to bring local drinkers out to the roadside, 1994.

The peloton dwarfed by the Pyrénées on the stage from Tarbes–Pau, 1995.

Above: Laurent Jalabert and Fabiano Fontanelli take stock after a multiple-rider pile up at Armentières, 1994. The crash had been caused by a policeman stepping out to take a photo of the riders. Note the oily chain imprint on Fontanelli's left cheek.

Opposite: Riders come to grief on the first stage of the 2002 Tour, in Luxembourg.

Above: Chris Boardman on his way to winning the Tour prologue in Dublin, 1998. The British rider became an expert at the Tour's first-day stages against the clock – this was his third win, after 1994 and 1997. His 1994 prologue remains the fastest average speed for a stage in the Tour, covering the 7.2 kilometre course at an average of 55.15kph.

Opposite: The publicity caravan: by the first Tours of the 21st century the procession of promotional floats and entertainments that precedes the riders involved 200 vehicles and took 45 minutes to pass roadside spectators.

The Tour peloton descending the high passes, July 2000.

Above: Richard Virenque with his soigneur Willy Voet, in 1995. Virenque won the polka-dotted 'King of the Mountains' jersey for four years in a row, from 1994 to 1997 and, in the absence of a home challenger for the overall title, became a national icon within France.

Opposite, top and bottom: In 1998 Virenque's world unravelled: on the way to the race start in Dublin, soigneur Voet was stopped by customs officers in Belgium. His car was found to be filled with banned doping products. The rest of the Tour was marred by police raids and rider protests, as the Tour organization struggled to come to terms with allegations of widespread doping. Virenque was the highest profile rider caught up in the scandal – giving a tearful press conference as he and his Festina team were kicked out of the Tour.

Opposite: Eventual race winner Marco Pantani and the rest of the peloton stage a sit-down protest over the treatment of fellow riders in 1998. The peloton were particularly incensed at riders from the TVM team being taken into custody by the French drugs squad. With the Festina team expelled, six other teams withdrew from the race, as a series of drug revelations disrupted the Tour.

Above: After the nadir of 1998, the Lance Armstrong story was just what the Tour was waiting for. Cancer survivor and four-time champion (to date), the Texan was a ready-made hero for the traumatized race. Armstrong won the so-called 'Tour of Redemption' in 1999 – and has never looked like losing since. He is shown here celebrating his 2000 win.

A rare bright spot for the peloton during the troubled 1998 Tour.

Opposite, top: Jan Ullrich, 1997 Tour champion, at Courchevel.

Opposite, bottom: Marco Pantani in 1998, on his way to becoming the first Italian to win the Tour for 33 years.

Above: Lance Armstrong and Marco Pantani on the Mont Ventoux stage of the 2000 Tour. The American golden boy and the Italian ex-champion – dogged by injury and controversy and anxious to prove that his day had not passed – enjoyed one of the great Tour duels that year. It was a duel that ranged from epic sporting struggle (with the now seemingly invincible Armstrong the eventual winner) to childish name-calling in the press – Armstrong renaming the self-styled 'Pirate' as 'Elefantino', in honour of his sizeable ears.

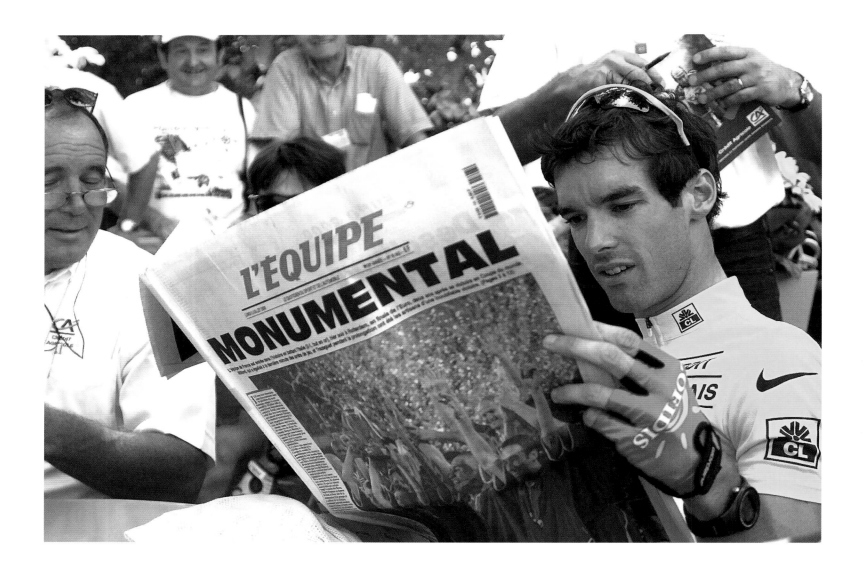

Above: Having won the 2000 Tour prologue on his first-ever day in the race, Britain's David Millar finds his yellow jersey competing for column inches with the French football team's European Championship triumph.

Opposite: The peloton on the fifth stage, from Vannes to Vitré, 2000.

Lance Armstrong passes through
Chalet Reynard ski station en route to
the summit of Mont Ventoux, July 2002.

Opposite, top: Felice Gimondi, Italian winner of the 1965 Tour de France, congratulates his belated successor, Marco Pantani, in 1998.

Opposite, bottom: Eddy Merckx and his son Axel, who was riding for the Domo team in the 2001 Tour.

Above: Lance Armstrong recruits film star and cycling überfan Robin Williams to the US Postal colours in 2002.

Armstrong in Paris. His victories took cycling into a new age, with the Texan invited to the White House, penning a bestselling autobiography and receiving multi-million dollar product endorsement contracts.

Statistics

YELLOW JERSEY
The jersey worn by the race leader (and eventual race winner) was, in fact, only introduced to the Tour in 1919. The traditional reason given for its colour is that it matched the pages of *L'Auto*, the newspaper that invented and ran the Tour – though less romantic accounts suggest that the decision was more influenced by the limited choice of colours available after the First World War.

1903
Maurice Garin (Fra)
1904
Henri Cornet (Fra)
1905
Louis Trousselier (Fra)
1906
René Pottier (Fra)
1907
Lucien Petit-Breton (Fra)
1908
Lucien Petit-Breton (Fra)
1909
François Faber (Lux)
1910
Octave Lapize (Fra)
1911
Gustave Garrigou (Fra)
1912
Odeil Defraye (Bel)
1913
Philippe Thys (Bel)
1914
Philippe Thys (Bel)
1919
Firmin Lambot (Bel)
1920
Philippe Thys (Bel)

1921
Léon Scieur (Bel)
1922
Firmin Lambot (Bel)
1923
Henri Pelissier (Fra)
1924
Ottavio Bottecchia (Ita)
1925
Ottavio Bottecchia (Ita)
1926
Lucien Buysse (Bel)
1927
Nicolas Frantz (Lux)
1928
Nicolas Frantz (Lux)
1929
Maurice Dewaele (Bel)
1930
André Leducq (Fra)
1931
Antonin Magne (Fra)
1932
André Leducq (Fra)
1933
Georges Speicher (Fra)
1934
Antonin Magne (Fra)
1935
Romain Maes (Bel)
1936
Sylvère Maes (Bel)
1937
Roger Lapébie (Fra)
1938
Gino Bartali (Ita)
1939
Sylvère Maes (Bel)
1947
Jean Robic (Fra)
1948
Gino Bartali (Ita)
1949
Fausto Coppi (Ita)
1950
Ferdi Kubler (Swi)

1951
Hugo Koblet (Swi)
1952
Fausto Coppi (Ita)
1953
Louison Bobet (Fra)
1954
Louison Bobet (Fra)
1955
Louison Bobet (Fra)
1956
Roger Walkowiak (Fra)
1957
Jacques Anquetil (Fra)
1958
Charly Gaul (Lux)
1959
Fed. Bahamontes (Spa)
1960
Gastone Nencini (Ita)
1961
Jacques Anquetil (Fra)
1962
Jacques Anquetil (Fra)
1963
Jacques Anquetil (Fra)
1964
Jacques Anquetil (Fra)
1965
Felice Gimondi (Ita)
1966
Lucien Aimar (Fra)
1967
Roger Pingeon (Fra)
1968
Jan Janssen (Hol)
1969
Eddy Merckx (Bel)
1970
Eddy Merckx (Bel)
1971
Eddy Merckx (Bel)
1972
Eddy Merckx (Bel)
1973
Luis Ocaña (Spa)

1974
Eddy Merckx (Bel)
1975
Bernard Thévenet (Fra)
1976
Lucien Van Impe (Bel)
1977
Bernard Thévenet (Fra)
1978
Bernard Hinault (Fra)
1979
Bernard Hinault (Fra)
1980
Joop Zoetemelk (Hol)
1981
Bernard Hinault (Fra)
1982
Bernard Hinault (Fra)
1983
Laurent Fignon (Fra)
1984
Laurent Fignon (Fra)
1985
Bernard Hinault (Fra)
1986
Greg LeMond (USA)
1987
Stephen Roche (Irl)
1988
Pedro Delgado (Spa)
1989
Greg LeMond (USA)
1990
Greg LeMond (USA)
1991
Miguel Indurain (Spa)
1992
Miguel Indurain (Spa)
1993
Miguel Indurain (Spa)
1994
Miguel Indurain (Spa)
1995
Miguel Indurain (Spa)
1996
Bjarne Riis (Den)

1997
Jan Uiirich (Ger)
1998
Marco Pantani (Ita)
1999
Lance Armstrong (USA)
2000
Lance Armstrong (USA)
2001
Lance Armstrong (USA)
2002
Lance Armstrong (USA)

GREEN JERSEY
First awarded in 1953, the green jersey is given to the Tour rider who wins the most points and is generally designed to reward sprinters. Points are given for final placings on a stage, but also for a series of 'intermediate' sprints en route. In this way, stages are punctuated by a series of lesser first-past-the-post sprints that form the core of the points competition.

1953
Fritz Schaer (Swi)
1954
Ferdi Kubler (Swi)
1955
Stan Ockers (Bel)
1956
Stan Ockers (Bel)
1957
Jean Forestier (Fra)
1958
Jean Graczyk (Fra)
1959
André Darrigade (Fra)
1960
Jean Graczyk (Fra)

1961
André Darrigade (Fra)
1962
Rudi Altig (Ger)
1963
Rik Van Looy (Bel)
1964
Jan Janssen (Hol)
1965
Jan Janssen (Hol)
1966
Willy Planckaert (Bel)
1967
Jan Janssen (Hol)
1968
Franco Bitossi (Ita)
1969
Eddy Merckx (Bel)
1970
Walter Godefroot (Bel)
1971
Eddy Merckx (Bel)
1972
Eddy Merckx (Bel)
1973
H. Van Springel (Bel)
1974
Patrick Sercu (Bel)
1975
Rik Van Linden (Bel)
1976
Freddy Maertens (Bel)
1977
Jacques Esclassan (Fra)
1978
Freddy Maertens (Bel)
1979
Bernard Hinault (Fra)
1980
Rudy Pevenage (Bel)
1981
Freddy Maertens (Bel)
1982
Sean Kelly (Irl)
1983
Sean Kelly (Irl)

1984
Frank Hoste (Bel)
1985
Sean Kelly (Irl)
1986
Eric Vanderaerden (Bel)
1987
J.P. Van Poppel (Hol)
1988
Eddy Planckaert (Bel)
1989
Sean Kelly (Irl)
1990
Olaf Ludwig (Ger)
1991
D Abdoujaparov (Uzb)
1992
Laurent Jalabert (Fra)
1993
D Abdoujaparov (Uzb)
1994
D Abdoujaparov (Uzb)
1995
Laurent Jalabert (Fra)
1996
Erik Zabel (Ger)
1997
Erik Zabel (Ger)
1998
Erik Zabel (Ger)
1999
Erik Zabel (Ger)
2000
Erik Zabel (Ger)
2001
Erik Zabel (Ger)
2002
Robbie McEwen (Aus)

KING OF THE MOUNTAINS JERSEY
The polka-dot jersey was first awarded in 1933 and goes to the climber who amasses the most points during the Tour. Different scales of points are awarded to the first 12 riders to reach the top of every climb throughout the Tour, with various factors taken into account to grade the climbs – from height and steepness to quality of road surface.

1933
Vicente Trueba (Spa)
1934
René Vietto (Fra)
1935
Félicien Vervaecke (Bel)
1936
Julian Berrendero (Spa)
1937
Félicien Vervaecke (Bel)
1938
Gino Bartali (Ita)
1939
Sylvere Maes (Bel)
1947
Pierre Brambilla (Ita)
1948
Gino Bartali (Ita)
1949
Fausto Coppi (Ita)
1950
Louison Bobet (Fra)
1951
Raphaël Geminiani (Fra)
1952
Fausto Coppi (Ita)
1953
Jesus Lorono (Spa)
1954
Fed. Bahamontes (Spa)
1955
Charly Gaul (Lux)
1956
Charly Gaul (Lux)
1957
Gastone Nencini (Ita)

1958
Fed. Bahamontes (Spa)
1959
Fed. Bahamontes (Spa)
1960
Imerio Massignan (Ita)
1961
Imerio Massignan (Ita)
1962
Fed. Bahamontes (Spa)
1963
Fed. Bahamontes (Spa)
1964
Fed. Bahamontes (Spa)
1965
Julio Jimenez (Spa)
1966
Julio Jimenez (Spa)
1967
Julio Jimenez (Spa)
1968
Aurelio Gonzalez (Spa)
1969
Eddy Merckx (Bel)
1970
Eddy Merckx (Bel)
1971
Lucien Van Impe (Bel)
1972
Lucien Van Impe (Bel)
1973
Pedro Torrès (Spa)
1974
Domingo Perurena (Spa)
1975
Lucien Van Impe (Bel)
1976
Giancarlo Bellini (Ita)
1977
Lucien Van Impe (Bel)
1978
Mariano Martinez (Fra)
1979
Giovanni Battaglin (Ita)
1980
Raymond Martin (Fra)

1981
Lucien Van Impe (Bel)
1982
Bernard Vallet (Fra)
1983
Lucien Van Impe (Bel)
1984
Robert Millar (GBR)
1985
Luis Herrera (Col)
1986
Bernard Hinault (Fra)
1987
Luis Herrera (Col)
1988
Steven Rooks (Hol)
1989
G.J. Theunisse (Hol)
1990
Thierry Claveyrolat (Fra)
1991
Claudio Chiappucci (Ita)
1992
Claudio Chiappucci (Ita)
1993
Tony Rominger (Swi)
1994
Richard Virenque (Fra)
1995
Richard Virenque (Fra)
1996
Richard Virenque (Fra)
1997
Richard Virenque (Fra)
1998
Christophe Rinero (Fra)
1999
Richard Virenque (Fra)
2000
Santiago Botero (Col)
2001
Laurent Jalabert (Fra)
2002
Laurent Jalabert (Fra)

Index

Picture Credits

Essential Works acknowledges the assistance provided by Paul Roberts and colleagues at Offside Sports Photography Limited. All pictures are supplied by Offside with the following exceptions:

ISO Sport: 248 (top and bottom), 249
John Pierce/Photosport International: 173, 202, 232
Cor Vos: 172, 226, 233, 234, 237 (top), 236, 240, 246

Acknowledgments

Author's Acknowledgments

For his wit, cameraderie and generally bright ideas, I would like to thank Duncan Steer. I also owe thanks for editorial support to Katie Cowan at Essential Works, to *procycling* magazine's inimitable team, and in addition, to Steven Hunter, Sally O'Sullivan, David Chappell and also Denis Descamps at ASO.

This book owes much to the steady supply of inspiration from a decade of Tour press packcolleagues, including Peter Cossins, Tim de Waele, Andrew Hood, Samuel Abt, Roger de Martelaere, Susanne Horsdal, Philippe Van Holle, Stephen Farrand, Mike Price, Rupert Guiness, Rob Arnold, Kirsten Begg, Pierre Ballester, Daniel Friebe, Matt Rendell, William Fotheringham, Andrew Longmore, Leon de Kort, David Sharp, John Deering, Freya North, Les Woodland – to name but a few.

Finally, thanks and much love to my parents, and to Debbie, Esme and Murf.

For Essential Works

Project Consultant: Duncan Steer
Design: Barbara Saulini and Liz Brown
Editor: Barbara Dixon
Index: Ian Crane